Lerner SPORTS™

FRANCE NATIONAL SOCCER TEAMS

ULTIMATE FAN GUIDE

KEITH ELLIOT GREENBERG

Lerner Publications ◆ Minneapolis

Lerner Publications Company
An imprint of Lerner Publishing Group, Inc.
241 First Avenue North
Minneapolis, MN 55401 USA

For reading levels and more information, look up this title at www.lernerbooks.com.

Main body text set in Aptifer Slab LT Pro.
Typeface provided by Linotype AG.

Editor: Evan Villas **Designer:** Viet Chu **Photo Editor:** Elena Mai
Lerner team: Martha Kranes

Library of Congress Cataloging-in-Publication Data

Names: Greenberg, Keith Elliot, 1959- author
Title: France national soccer teams : ultimate fan guide / Keith Elliot Greenberg.
Description: Minneapolis : Lerner Publications, [2026] | Series: Lerner sports. World Cup fan guides | Includes bibliographical references and index. | Audience: Ages 7–11 | Audience: Grades 2–3 | Summary: "With talented women like Wendie Renard and superstar men like Kylian Mbappé, the French national soccer team has never been stronger. Discover the history and greatest moments of this legendary team"— Provided by publisher.
Identifiers: LCCN 2025011897 (print) | LCCN 2025011898 (ebook) | ISBN 9798765689394 lib. bdg. | ISBN 9798348029319 pbk | ISBN 9798765698662 epub
Subjects: LCSH: Soccer players—France—History | Soccer teams—France—History
Classification: LCC GV944.F8 G74 2026 (print) | LCC GV944.F8 (ebook) | DDC 796.334/660944—dc23/eng/20250717

LC record available at https://lccn.loc.gov/2025011897
LC ebook record available at https://lccn.loc.gov/2025011898

Manufactured in the United States of America
1-1012737-54807-8/7/2025

TABLE OF CONTENTS

Kylian Mbappé (*left*) celebrates his goal at the 2018 Men's World Cup final with his teammates.

INTRODUCTION

AN AMAZING MEMORY

The 2018 Men's World Cup had come down to two teams. France and Croatia were battling for soccer's biggest prize. France scored its first goal when Croatian striker Mario Mandžukić knocked the ball into his own net by mistake. Croatia's Ivan Perišić tied the game 10 minutes later.

France's Antoine Griezmann scored before halftime to put his team ahead 2–1. In the 59th minute, his teammate Paul Pogba brought the score to 3–1. Then France's young star Kylian Mbappé kicked the ball into the net. At 19, he was the second teenager to ever score in a World Cup final. The first was Brazil's Pelé in 1958.

Croatia did their best to get back into the game. Putting his early mistake behind him, Mandžukić booted the ball past France's goalkeeper to bring the score to 4–2. The French responded with a perfect display of their "Iron Wall" defense. Croatia was unable to score the rest of the game.

FAST FACTS

France's Lucien Laurent scored the first goal in the first-ever Men's World Cup in 1930.

The French men's team won a World Cup and European Championship back-to-back in 1998 and 2000.

When France hosted the 2019 Women's World Cup, more than a million fans attended the games.

Wendie Renard joined the French women's national team when she was 16.

Fans in Paris, France, celebrate the French men's team beating Croatia in the 2018 World Cup final.

When the game ended, people around France jumped up and down in the street. They screamed and sang their national anthem. The sounds of cars honking and fireworks exploding filled the air.

French fans carry the memory of that day as their country's men's and women's teams compete for World Cup, Olympic, and Union of European Football

Associations (UEFA) titles. These tournaments take place every four years. French fans look forward to great victories. But they also appreciate the history that helped turn their men's and women's teams into some of the best in the world.

The French men's national team celebrates winning the 2018 World Cup.

The French men's national soccer team attends the 1924 Summer Olympics.

CHAPTER 1

INSPIRING THE COUNTRY

Although a French men's national soccer team appeared in the 1900 Olympics, the players went their separate ways afterward. In 1904, an official team was formed. In their first international match, the French tied Belgium 3–3.

France's Lucien Laurent scored the first goal in the first-ever World Cup in 1930. France beat Mexico 4–1.

The team reached the quarterfinals but lost to Italy. A long rivalry with the Italians began. Over time, the French men formed rivalries with other teams including Germany, Spain, Brazil, and Argentina.

The French men's national soccer team before their match against Mexico in the 1930 World Cup

During the men's team's early years, it was difficult for Black athletes to play in France. They were barred from joining the national soccer team for many years. The first Black player to play for the French national team was Raoul Diagne. He made the team in 1931. Diagne's family was from Senegal in Africa. He helped pave the way for future players such as Thierry Henry and Kylian Mbappé.

Raoul Diagne (*top left*) with teammates in 1937

The French women's national team plays a game in London, England, in 1920.

French women have been competing in international soccer games since the 1920s. But the country's interest in their matches didn't last. In 1932, a league that included women's teams from all over the country was shut down. The government even banned women's soccer afterward.

The French women's national soccer team heads to Mexico for the World Cup in 1971.

In 1970, a new women's national team was created. Women's soccer players were finally able to represent France. The French women had dramatic matches against teams from around the world such as Brazil and the United States.

DRESSED FOR SUCCESS

In 1978, players for France and Hungary both showed up for a Men's World Cup game in Argentina wearing white uniforms. To avoid confusion, France played in green-and-white-striped shirts borrowed from a local team.

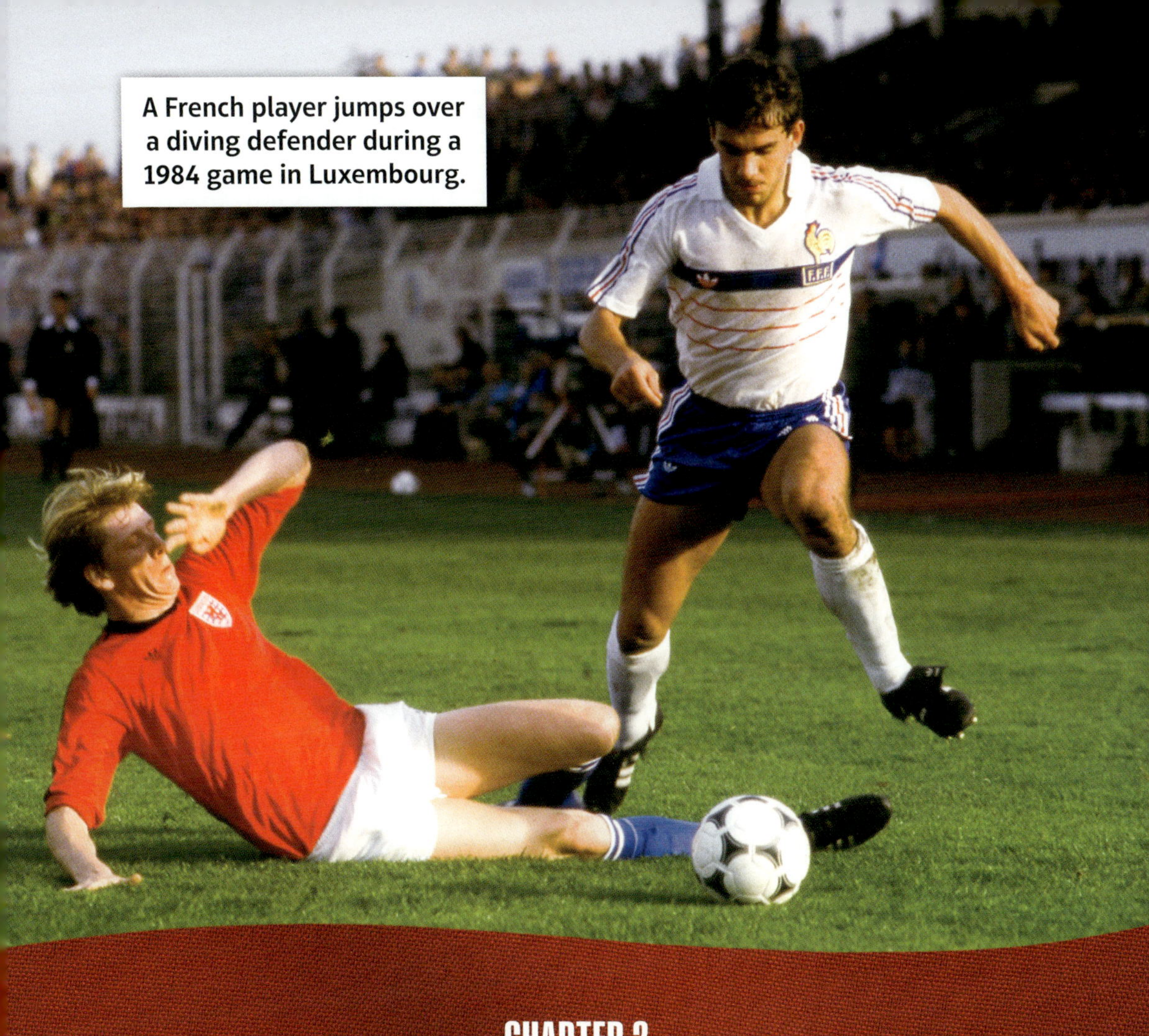
A French player jumps over a diving defender during a 1984 game in Luxembourg.

CHAPTER 2

GOLDEN YEARS

French men's soccer boomed in the 1980s. In 1984, the team won its first Olympic gold medal. They defeated Brazil 2–0 in the final with goals from François Brisson and Daniel Xuereb.

That year, France hosted and won the UEFA European Championship. Team Captain Michel Platini scored nine goals in five games. This set a European Championship record that stood for almost 40 years. Platini was part of an exciting group of players including Alain Giresse, Jean Tigana, and Luis Fernandez.

UEFA held the first European Championship for women in 1984, but France didn't qualify. They also

Michel Platini (*right*) attempts to steal the ball from a Spanish player during the European Championship final in 1984.

Zinedine Zidane (*center*) playing in the first round of the 1998 Men's World Cup

didn't qualify in 1987. In 1989, they lost to Italy in the quarterfinals of the qualifying round. France did not qualify for the championship until 1997.

France's next group of great men's players was led by Zinedine Zidane. The son of immigrants from Algeria, Zidane made his first appearance for the French men's team in 1994. He was praised for his free-flowing style and ballhandling. Zidane had an amazing career. He was named World Player of the Year in 1998, 2000, and 2003.

DOING IT ALL

Didier Deschamps is one of the few people to win the World Cup both as a player (in 1998) and coach (in 2018).

France's men's team celebrates winning the World Cup in 1998.

France won its first Men's World Cup in 1998. They beat soccer powerhouse Brazil 3–0 in the final after two goals from Zidane. The World Cup win sent France into a frenzy. More than a million people celebrated the win in the streets of Paris.

Two years later, the French beat a tough Italian team 2–1 in the UEFA European Championship finals. They did what few teams do. They won a World Cup and European Championship back-to-back.

Meanwhile, the women's team was slowly building a following. Starting in 2000, more and more talented players were drawn to the team. The French reached the European Championship quarterfinals in 2001 and 2005. In 2003, the team qualified for its first World Cup.

Four French women's team players celebrating at the 2005 European Championship

Marco Materazzi (*second from right*) scores a goal during the 2006 World Cup final.

Three years later, the French men were matched against Italy in the World Cup final. Zidane and Italy's Marco Materazzi were the stars of the game. Each scored a goal. Tensions ran high between the two rivals.

The game was tied 1–1 in extra time. Materazzi and Zidane exchanged words as they ran up the field. Materazzi insulted Zidane, who then headbutted his rival in the chest. Zidane received a red card and had to leave the game. Materazzi later apologized, and Zidane said that he was not proud of what took place.

The score was still tied at the end of extra time, so the game was decided on penalty kicks. Italy won 5–3 and became World Cup champions. Zidane retired soon after and became a successful coach.

In 2009, the French women's team was captained by Sandrine Soubeyrand. It featured other talented players such as Laura Georges, Corine Franco, and Camille Abily. Under Coach Bruno Bini, the team made it to the knockout stage of the UEFA European Championship. But they lost on penalty kicks to the Netherlands.

Sandrine Soubeyrand (*top*) and Germany's Simone Laudehr fight for the ball during a match in 2009.

The team took fourth place in the 2011 Women's World Cup. They also placed fourth in the 2012 Olympics. In the 2015 World Cup, they made it to the quarterfinals.

Meanwhile, the French men's team continued to excel. While hosting the European Championship in 2016, France defeated Ireland, Iceland, and Germany. The team lost 1–0 to Portugal in the final, but fans were satisfied with the team's performance.

France (*blue jerseys*) facing Portugal at the 2016 European Championship final

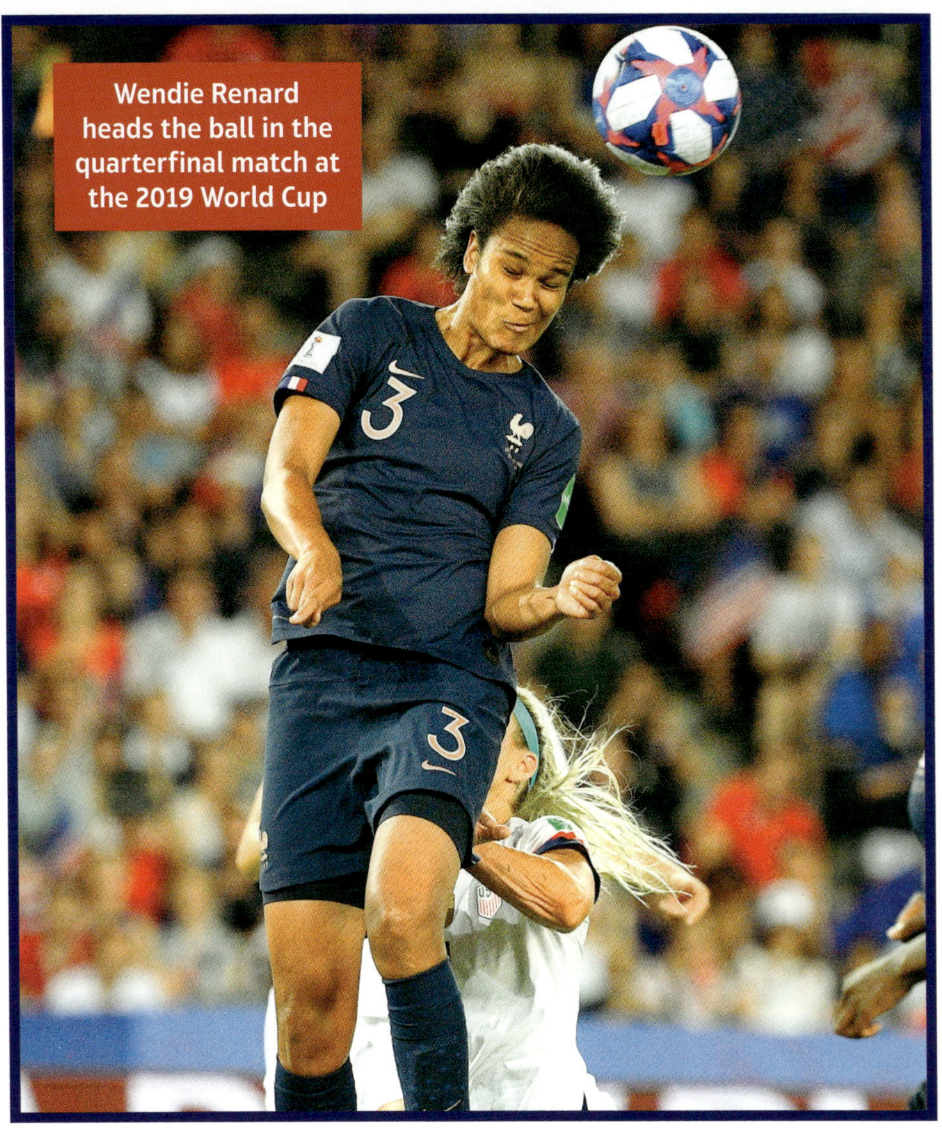
Wendie Renard heads the ball in the quarterfinal match at the 2019 World Cup

When France hosted the 2019 Women's World Cup, more than a million fans attended the games. France lost to the United States 2–1 in the quarterfinals. More than 45,000 people packed into the stadium to watch the game.

French players practice at the National Center of Football in 2024.

CHAPTER 3

A BLEUE WAVE

The French men and women both train at the country's special soccer school, the National Center of Football. The school is near Paris in Clairefontaine. The school also prepares coaches and referees.

The women do not have their own stadium, but the men play most of their home games at the national field in Saint-Denis. The stadium seats more than 80,000 fans. When the teams travel, thousands of people turn out to cheer on Les Bleues. The team's nickname means "the Blues."

The French men's team at the National Center of Football in 2025

CHANGING THE WORLD

The French training school is so respected that its coaches have helped organize soccer programs for other countries. These include China, the United Arab Emirates, and the United States.

Fans were overjoyed when the men's team made the World Cup final in 2022 for the second time in a row. The team lost to Argentina in a penalty kick shootout. But fans still praised their performance.

France fans cheer on their favorite team at a 2024 match.

Didier Deschamps (*second from left*) speaks with other coaches during a training session at the National Center of Football in 2025.

The men have been coached by former star player Didier Deschamps since 2012. He said that his job is made easier by having a team of great competitors. These include forward Kylian Mbappé, midfielder Eduardo Camavinga, and goalkeeper Mike Maignan.

Laurent Bonadei became the head coach of the women's team in 2024. Captain Wendie Renard is a vocal leader. She's been on the team since she was 16. The women's team boasts some of its best players ever. These

Laurent Bonadei (*front left*) speaks with players during a match in 2025.

Wendie Renard (*right*) celebrates her goal during a 2025 match.

include forwards Eugénie Le Sommer and Kadidiatou Diani, goalkeeper Constance Picaud, and midfielder Grace Geyoro.

French fans are eager to see their teams win it all. Each tournament brings high expectations. Talented new players give fans hope for the future.

FRANCE MEN'S TEAM TIMELINE

1904 The French national soccer team is founded.

1930 France wins its first World Cup game, beating Mexico 4–1.

1984 France wins the UEFA European Championship for the first time, defeating Spain 2–0 in the final.

1998 France wins its first World Cup, topping Brazil 3–0.

2000 France wins its second UEFA European Championship with its 2–1 overtime win over Italy.

2006 France reaches the World Cup final but loses to Italy on penalty kicks.

2018 France becomes World Cup champions for the second time, beating Croatia 4–2.

2022 France reaches the World Cup final again but loses to Argentina on penalty kicks.

FRANCE WOMEN'S TEAM TIMELINE

1920 A group of French women play their first international game, losing 2–0 to a British team.

1932 Organized women's soccer is banned in France.

1970 A new national women's team is created.

2003 France qualifies for the Women's World Cup for the first time.

2011 France takes fourth place in the Women's World Cup.

2012 For the first time, the French women's soccer team appears in the Olympics, coming in fourth place.

2015 France reaches the quarterfinals of the Women's World Cup.

2019 Nine French cities host the Women's World Cup. France's quarterfinal loss to the United States sets an attendance record.

GLOSSARY

extra time: time added to the end of a game

forward: a player whose main job is to score goals

knockout stage: the part of a tournament in which a losing team is eliminated

midfielder: a player who plays around the middle of the field

penalty kick: a free kick at the goal allowed for certain fouls or to break a tie

qualify: to be allowed to play in a tournament

quarterfinal: the round of a tournament to determine the four final teams

red card: a red card that a referee holds in the air when a player who has broken the rules will not be allowed to continue playing

rival: an opponent

tournament: a series of games played to determine a champion

LEARN MORE

Britannica Kids: Zinedine Zidane
https://kids.britannica.com/scholars/article/Zinedine-Zidane/442462

Jökulsson, Illugi. *Stars of Women's Soccer.* Abbeville, 2021.

Kiddle: France National Football Team Facts for Kids
https://kids.kiddle.co/France_national_football_team

Kiddle: France Women's National Football Team Facts for Kids
https://kids.kiddle.co/France_women%27s_national_football_team

Moon, Derek. *Kylian Mbappé.* Press Box Books, 2025.

Scheff, Matt. *The World Cup.* Lerner Publications, 2021.

INDEX

PHOTO ACKNOWLEDGMENTS

Image credits: Marvin Ibo Guengoer/picture-alliance/dpa/AP Images, p. 4; Aurore Marechal/Abaca/Sipa USA, p. 6; Kunihiko Miura/The Yomiuri Shimbun via AP Image, p. 7; Popperfoto via Getty Images, p. 8; Bob Thomas/Popperfoto via Getty Images/Getty Images, p. 9; The Picture Art Collection/Alamy, p. 10; Firmin/Topical Press Agency/Hulton Archive/Getty Images, p. 11; MARCEL BINH/AFP via Getty Images, p. 12; Alain de Martignac/Onze/Icon Sport/Getty Images, p. 13; Trevor Jones/Allsport/Getty Images/Hulton Archive, p. 14; Simon Bruty/Anychance/Getty Image, p. 15; Eric Renard/Onze/Icon Sport, p. 16; PA Images/Alamy, p. 17; Stewart Kendall/Sportsphoto/Allstar via Getty Images, p. 18; CARMEN JASPERSEN/dpa picture alliance/Alamy, p. 19; Nolwenn Le Gouic/ Icon Sport via Getty Images/Getty Images, p. 20; Christian Liewig/Abaca/Sipa via AP Images, p. 21; Anthony Bibard/FEP/Icon Sport/Sipa via AP Images, p. 22; J.E.E/SIPA via AP Images, p. 23; Foto Olimpik/NurPhoto via AP Imanges, p. 24; CHRISTOPHE SAIDI/Sipa via AP Images, p. 25; Baptiste Fernandez/Icon Sport via Getty Images, p. 26; Eurasia Sport Images/Getty Images, p. 27. Design elements: Ralf Hiemisch/Getty Images; Rifqyhsn Design/Getty Images; cunfek/Getty Images; poo worawit/Getty Images.

Cover: Cal Sport Media via AP Images (left); AP Photo/Thibault Camus (right).